ENGINEERING WONDERS

THE GOLDEN GATE BRIDGE

BY REBECCA STANBOROUGH

CAPSTONE PRESS
a capstone imprint

Fact Finders Books are published by Capstone Press,
1710 Roe Crest Drive, North Mankato, Minnesota 56003
www.capstonepub.com

Library of Congress Cataloging-in-Publication Data
Names: Stanborough, Rebecca, author.
Title: The Golden Gate Bridge / by Rebecca Stanborough.
Other titles: Fact finders. Engineering wonders.
Description: North Mankato, Minnesota : Capstone Press, [2016] | Series: Fact
    finders. Engineering wonders | Audience: Ages 8–10. | Audience: Grades 4
    to 6. | Includes bibliographical references and index.
Identifiers: LCCN 2015039680
    ISBN 978-1-4914-8196-7 (library binding)
    ISBN 978-1-4914-8200-1 (pbk.)
    ISBN 978-1-4914-8204-9 (ebook pdf)
Subjects: LCSH: Golden Gate Bridge (San Francisco, Calif.)—Juvenile
    literature. | Golden Gate Bridge (San Francisco, Calif.)—Design and
    construction—History—Juvenile literature. | Bridges—California—San
    Francisco—Design and construction—Juvenile literature.
Classification: LCC TG25.S225 S735 2016 | DDC 624.2/30979461—dc23
LC record available at http://lccn.loc.gov/2015039680

Editorial Credits
Elizabeth Johnson and Gena Chester, editors; Veronica Scott, designer;
Svetlana Zhurkin, media researcher; Lori Barbeau, production specialist

Photo Credits
Alamy: Sueddeutsche Zeitung Photo, 25; California Historical Society, CHS2011.734, 10;
Corbis, 8, San Francisco Chronicle, 24; Dreamstime: Gavin Duncan, 11 (middle); Getty Images:
Underwood Archives, cover, 13 (top), 19, 20, 22; iStockphoto: narvikk, 27; Library of Congress,
6, 7, 9, 14, 16; NASA, 4; National Parks Service: Fort Point-Golden Gate, 18; Newscom: UIG/
Underwood Archives, 23; Shutterstock: Creative Stall, 13 (bottom), Dr_Flash, 21 (bottom left),
Jozsef Bagota, 21 (bottom middle and right), leungchopan, 11 (bottom), Luciano Mortula, 5,
pmphoto, 28 (top), Robert Cicchetti, 11 (top), Stas Moroz, 28—29, Steve Buckley, 26, topseller, 21
(middle right); SuperStock: Underwood Photo Archives, 15

Design Elements by Shutterstockww

Printed in the United States of America, in North Mankato.
007539CGS16

TABLE OF CONTENTS

CHAPTER 1

FLOODS OF WATER, FLOODS OF PEOPLE

The Golden Gate Bridge is known for its beauty. Its bright orange color stands out against the blue bay and sky. Its sweeping cables and airy towers echo the rise and fall of the mountains. But this beauty of a bridge is also strong. It weighs nearly 877,000 tons (795,601 metric tons) and carries the weight of over 112,000 cars and trucks every day. Best of all, the Golden Gate Bridge moves. To respond to the Bay Area's fierce winds and earthquakes, this bridge was built to bounce. How did this steel and concrete wonder come to be?

The San Francisco Bay photographed from the *Columbia* Space Shuttle.

4

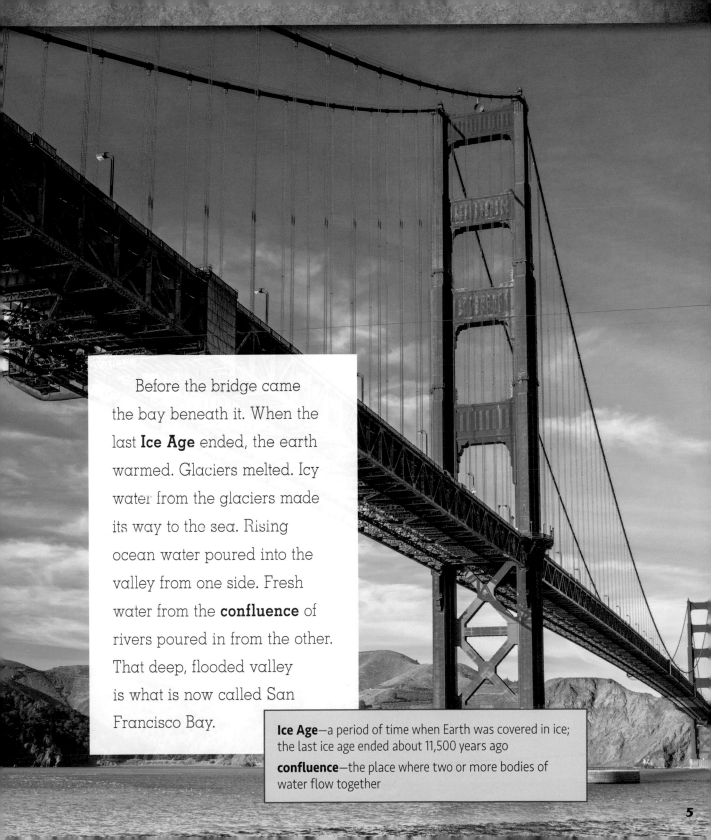

Before the bridge came the bay beneath it. When the last **Ice Age** ended, the earth warmed. Glaciers melted. Icy water from the glaciers made its way to the sea. Rising ocean water poured into the valley from one side. Fresh water from the **confluence** of rivers poured in from the other. That deep, flooded valley is what is now called San Francisco Bay.

Ice Age—a period of time when Earth was covered in ice; the last ice age ended about 11,500 years ago

confluence—the place where two or more bodies of water flow together

SETTLERS ALONG THE SHORE

The bay waters were home to fish and shellfish. The climate was mild and the woods were full of elk and other animals. Ohlone, Coast Miwok, and Patwin people enjoyed the natural resources for many generations.

In 1775, Spanish explorer Juan Manuel de Ayala sailed the *San Carlos* into the bay. Within 150 years of the Spanish arrival, the Ohlone, Coast Miwok, and Patwin people were almost gone. Then someone made a discovery that would bring a different kind of flood to the Bay Area—a cascade of new settlers. That discovery was gold.

WHY IS IT CALLED THE "GOLDEN GATE"?

In 1846, just before the **Gold Rush**, explorer John C. Frémont mapped the entrance to San Francisco Bay. He called the narrow opening *Chrysopylae*, or "Golden Gate" in Greek. He believed that the bay would become a thriving harbor one day. It would become a portal through which wealth and trade would pour into the nation.

Gold Rush!
In 1848, James Marshall found gold nuggets in water leading to California's American River. When news got out, people poured in from all over the world. In 1848, fewer than 1,000 people lived in San Francisco. Two years later, 20 times that many had arrived. By 1920, the population was over half a million people.

Gold Rush—the sudden arrival of crowds of people in search of gold

A NEW WAY TO TRAVEL

All those new Californians needed to get from one place to another. Dusty trails became roads. As more and more people settled in the Bay Area, traffic increased. People needed to get from the city of San Francisco to the houses and businesses in Marin County. The only way to cross the bay was by **ferry**. People drove their cars onto a ferry boat. The ferry boat crossed the Golden Gate. Then, the cars drove off the ferry and into Marin County. At peak times, the wait for a ferry could be three hours long.

Passengers ride a ferry across the bay.

ferry—a boat or ship that regularly carries people across a stretch of water

People cooking on the street after the earthquake and fire of 1906.

EARTHQUAKE!

On April 18, 1906, disaster struck. A massive earthquake hit San Francisco. Many of the houses, offices, schools, churches, and hospitals collapsed. Two-thirds of the city's people were left homeless. San Franciscans had to rebuild. Many of them wanted to include a bridge over the bay in rebuilding plans.

CHAPTER 2

A DESIGN THAT WORKS

AN UNPOPULAR FIRST DESIGN

In 1919, city officials asked San Francisco's chief **engineer**, Michael O'Shaughnessy, to find out whether a bridge could be built across the Golden Gate **Strait**. A Chicago engineer and bridge builder named Joseph Strauss believed the answer was "yes." Strauss proposed a bridge that would use two different kinds of support—cantilevers and suspension cables. City officials considered his design. Strauss also talked to the people of San Francisco. Many of them wanted a bridge, but some thought his design was ugly. "It looks like an upside-down rat trap," one critic said.

engineer—a person who uses science and mathematics to design, build, or maintain machines, buildings, or public works

strait—a narrow channel of water that connects two larger bodies of water

TYPES OF BRIDGES

A CANTILEVER BRIDGE has a central beam and supporting pillars. Metal trusses help distribute the weight of the vehicles crossing the deck of the bridge. The Ed Koch Queensboro Bridge in New York is a double-decker cantilever bridge.

A BASULE BRIDGE, sometimes called a "drawbridge," is a movable bridge with a single or double "leaf" that lifts to allow boat traffic to pass underneath. The Johnson Street Bridge, spanning the harbor in Victoria, British Columbia, was designed by Joseph Strauss.

A SUSPENSION BRIDGE uses vertical cables to hold up the roadway. Long supporting cables are draped over towers and anchored to concrete or to bedrock on either end of the bridge. Today, the longest suspension bridge in the world is the Akashi Kaikyo Bridge in Japan. Its total suspension is 12,828 feet (3,910 meters).

GENIUS!

A bridge as amazing as the Golden Gate was the work of many minds.

- Joseph Strauss was the bridge's champion. He surrounded himself with talented advisors.

- Leon Mouisseiff was a bridge designer from Latvia. He knew how to design strong, elegant towers out of flexible steel.

- Othmar Ammann was a Swiss engineer. He designed six of New York's most remarkable bridges.

- Charles Derleth, Jr. was an expert on building in the Bay Area.

- Andrew Lawson was a **geologist**. He knew more than almost anyone else about the **bedrock** and earthquakes of the region.

- John Eberson and Irving Morrow were both architects. They would make the Golden Gate Bridge one of the most dramatic bridges in the world.

- Charles Alton Ellis was the mathematical mind behind the bridge. Everyone wanted the bridge to be lighter and more graceful than other suspension bridges. But the bridge also had to be longer and stronger than the others. Ellis had to use math to test the strength and flexibility of the bridge. For 20 months, he calculated and recalculated.

geologist—someone who studies minerals, rocks, and soil
bedrock—a layer of solid rock beneath the layers of soil and loose gravel broken up by weathering

THE FORCES THAT STRESS A BRIDGE

Bridges have to be able to bear two types of loads: dead loads and live loads. First, every bridge has to be strong enough to bear the weight of its own materials. That weight is called the "dead" load. Second, every bridge has to be able to bear the weight of whatever is crossing the bridge. That weight is called the "live" load. Live loads also include water droplets and wind forces. Loads either push the parts of the bridge together (compression) or pull them apart (tension). The Golden Gate Bridge handles these forces two ways: the towers bear the compression forces, and the cables bear the tension forces.

CHAPTER 3

CONSTRUCTION BEGINS

THE WORK FORCE

It was difficult to design the bridge. But it would be even more difficult to build it. Fortunately, there was no shortage of able workers. When construction began in 1933, the country was deep in **the Depression**. Jobs were hard to find. People came from far away to compete for jobs on the bridge crew. Pay was very good because bridge workers faced danger every day.

PAID FOR
TO THIS POINT
Every Dollar
FROM YOUR
70 More Meals

the Depression—the Great Depression was the deepest and longest-lasting economic downturn in the history of the Western industrialized world

A worker walking up an incomplete bridge as winds blow around him. According to the U.S. National Weather Service, gale force winds blow steadily between 39-54 miles (63-87 kilometers) per hour.

Gale force winds bullied them as they hammered and welded 500 feet (152 m) off the ground. When fog rolled in, they could barely see. Water droplets made every step slick. And it was very cold up on the catwalks. Some workers even got lead poisoning from the **primer** paint used on the steel. Once, a small earthquake struck during the workday. Everyone grabbed the beams to keep from being thrown off the bridge.

primer—a base coat of paint that goes on before the main color

Even with all these dangers, people needed the work. Men lined up on the ground every day—waiting for someone to be injured so they could step in. Most workers had to belong to a **union** to get one of the bridge jobs. While unions helped members who worked get decent pay, only a select few received membership. Unions of that era were not open to minorities. Very few women or racial and ethnic minorities worked on the bridge.

Howard Street, also known as Skid Row, was the district where many of San Francisco's poor and unemployed people lived.

ANCHORING THE BRIDGE

The first step was to test the strength of the bedrock at the bottom of the bay. They needed to be sure the towers would stay in place. Geologists drilled holes in the bedrock. They looked at the **density** of the stone. They found that it was solid enough to hold up the towers.

Then work could begin on the two concrete **anchorages**. On the north end of the bridge, workers drove steel into the bedrock to make a frame. Then they poured 182,000 cubic yards (139,149 cubic meters) of concrete into the frame. The hard concrete would form the base to hold the towers.

The south anchorage was harder to build. It had to be located 1,125 feet (343 m) off shore, in the churning bay. Divers worked in the freezing water. They dove 100 feet (30.5 m) below the surface. They blasted holes in the bedrock using explosives. They worked in 20-minute shifts in the dark. They worked against the fierce pull of the tides.

union—a group of workers who try to gain more rights, such as fair pay and safer jobs, for workers

density—the amount of mass an object or substance has based on a unit of volume

anchorages—something that provides a secure hold; a massive masonry or concrete construction securing a cable at each end

Once the divers had blasted wells for the foundation, builders made a moat-like structure. They pumped out the seawater. Workers now had a dry area in which to build the rest of the anchorage. With the seawater gone, they could attach the steel foundation to bedrock. Then they poured in 130,000 cubic yards (99,392 cu m) of concrete. Together, the north and south anchorages support the towers and the cables that hold up the whole bridge.

Two workers sitting atop the Main Tower, 746 feet (227 m) above the water.

BUILDING THE TOWERS

Each of the two towers rises 746 feet (227 m) above the waterline. They appear to be made of solid steel. But the towers are made of hollow, beehive-like cells. Each cell is a 3½ foot (1 m) square. The towers can sway in all four directions in response to wind, temperature changes, and earthquakes.

To build the towers, workers stood on **scaffolds**. They had to be raised each time a new level was built. A total of 404 cells were connected with over 600,000 **rivets** in each tower. Two steel "saddles" sit atop each tower to hold the cables. Altogether, the towers contain 44,000 tons (39,916 mt) of steel.

Did You Know?

Inside the towers, there are 23 miles (37 km) of ladders and an elevator running top to bottom.

scaffolds—temporary framework or platforms used to support workers and materials
rivets—a short steel bolt that fastens two pieces of metal together

INTERNATIONAL ORANGE

Everyone had an opinion about what color the bridge should be painted. Some people wanted classic gray. Others worried that ships would not see a gray bridge in the fog. The U.S. Navy wanted yellow and black stripes so the bridge would be highly visible. The Army Air Corps rallied for red and white stripes. In the end, the bridge designers chose International Orange, a color very close to the red primer paint that covered the steel during construction. International Orange, they felt, would contrast with the blue sky and call attention to the natural beauty of the hills.

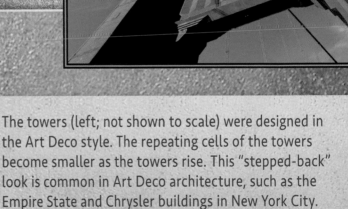

The towers (left; not shown to scale) were designed in the Art Deco style. The repeating cells of the towers become smaller as the towers rise. This "stepped-back" look is common in Art Deco architecture, such as the Empire State and Chrysler buildings in New York City. This style appears light and graceful. The towers could be both light and strong because of advances in steelwork.

CHAPTER 4

SPANNING THE BAY

DRAPING THE CABLES

The cables are not solid ropes of steel. They are woven of over 80,000 miles (128,747 km) of steel strands. Because of their weight, the cables had to be spun together on site, in the air. The steel workers used a kind of loom to twist the wires together in bundles. In each cable, there are 61 bundles. In each bundle, there are 452 wires. Once the cables were assembled, they were clamped with iron bands and wrapped in wire **sheaths** to protect the surface. Then they were draped over the towers and anchored in place. Each of the cables is around 3 feet (1 m) in diameter and 7,650 feet (2,332 m) long.

sheaths—a close-fitting cover for something, especially something that is elongated

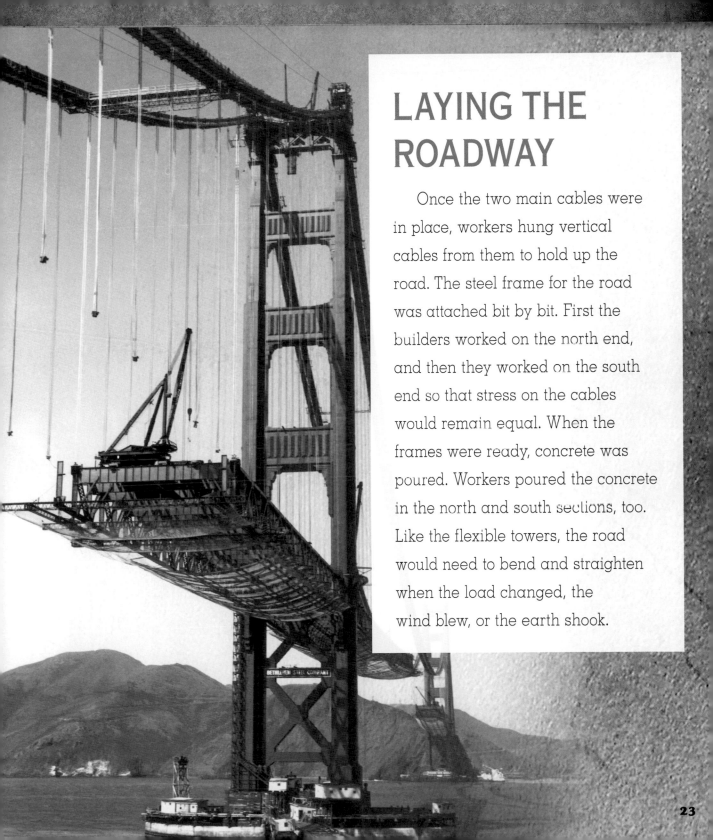

LAYING THE ROADWAY

Once the two main cables were in place, workers hung vertical cables from them to hold up the road. The steel frame for the road was attached bit by bit. First the builders worked on the north end, and then they worked on the south end so that stress on the cables would remain equal. When the frames were ready, concrete was poured. Workers poured the concrete in the north and south sections, too. Like the flexible towers, the road would need to bend and straighten when the load changed, the wind blew, or the earth shook.

WORKING SAFELY

Joseph Strauss and construction engineer Russell Cone wanted to make sure that workers stayed safe. For the first time on any construction site in the nation, workers were required to wear hard hats. When steel workers became sick from lead dust, they were given masks to keep the dust out of their lungs. They also wore special goggles that cut down on the glare from the sun and the sea. Most importantly, Strauss purchased a net that cost $130,000. He strung it up beneath the bridge. The net saved nineteen men from being killed when they fell.

Accidents still happened. One man, Kermit Moore, was crushed by a beam. And on February 17, 1937, ten men died when their scaffold collapsed and tore through the net. Their names are engraved on a plaque on the south end of the bridge.

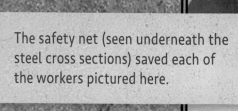

The safety net (seen underneath the steel cross sections) saved each of the workers pictured here.

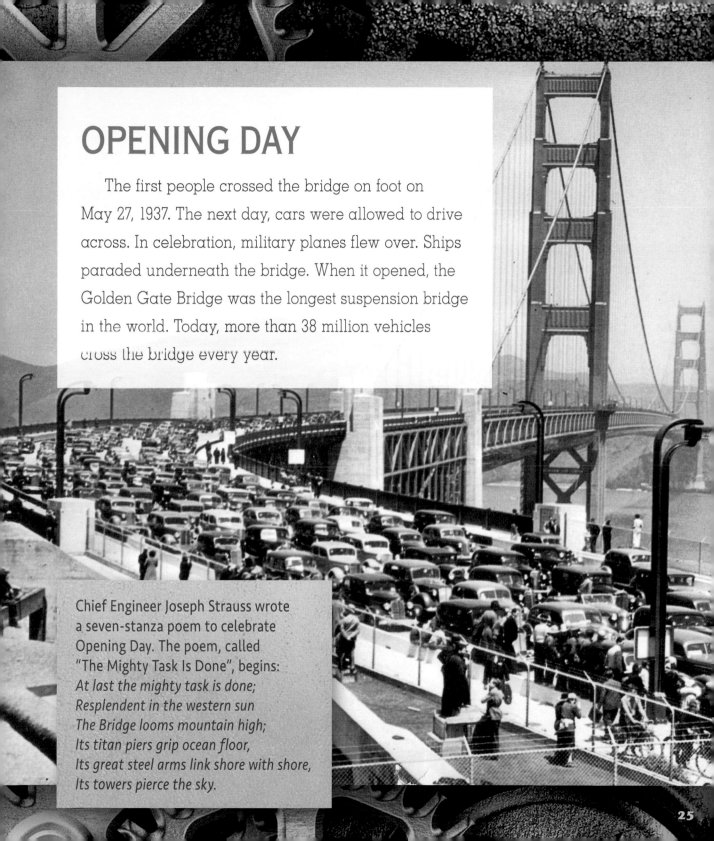

OPENING DAY

The first people crossed the bridge on foot on May 27, 1937. The next day, cars were allowed to drive across. In celebration, military planes flew over. Ships paraded underneath the bridge. When it opened, the Golden Gate Bridge was the longest suspension bridge in the world. Today, more than 38 million vehicles cross the bridge every year.

Chief Engineer Joseph Strauss wrote a seven-stanza poem to celebrate Opening Day. The poem, called "The Mighty Task Is Done", begins:

At last the mighty task is done;
Resplendent in the western sun
The Bridge looms mountain high;
Its titan piers grip ocean floor,
Its great steel arms link shore with shore,
Its towers pierce the sky.

CHAPTER 5

ACROSS THE BAY, ACROSS THE YEARS

CHANGING WITH THE TIMES

In 1951, high winds forced the bridge to close. After the storm passed, inspectors checked the bridge. They decided to add more **bracing** to make the bridge safer. Twice more, in 1982 and 1983, the bridge had to be closed when storms brought winds of more than 70 miles (113 km) per hour. The bridge was not damaged, thanks to the earlier bracing.

Repairs done in 2007

bracing—ties and rods used for supporting and strengthening various parts of a building

In 1989, the Loma Prieta earthquake ripped through San Francisco. It caused 68 deaths and millions of dollars in damage to buildings. The earthquake started 60 miles (97 km) away, so the bridge was not damaged. Engineers decided to **retrofit** the bridge anyway, in case a major earthquake struck closer.

retrofit—to provide something with new parts that were not available when it was originally built

Did You Know?

In 1977, the bridge was 40 years old. The roadway was cracking. The cracks were filled with salt used to de-ice the road. Engineers worried that the salt would eat into the steel, so the roadway was replaced. The new road was stronger—and thousands of tons lighter.

The Golden Gate Bridge means a lot to San Francisco and the United States. Engineers continue to make changes to keep it in safe working order. Salt, fog, wind, earthquakes, and other forces can damage the bridge. It is constantly being examined, repaired, and repainted.

Anchored deep in the earth, soaring into the sky, the Golden Gate Bridge is a wonder of engineering. It took a talented team of engineers to design a bridge that could bear such massive loads so gracefully. And it took many other people to make those designs a reality. The parts of the bridge itself—trusses, cables, towers, and anchorages—pull together to create safe passage for thousands of people crossing San Francisco Bay every day.

GLOSSARY

anchorage (ANK-or-ij)—something that provides a secure hold; a massive masonry or concrete construction securing a cable at each end

bedrock (BED-rok)—a layer of solid rock beneath the layers of soil and loose gravel broken up by weathering

bracing (BRAY-sing)—ties and rods used for supporting and strengthening various parts of a building

confluence (KON-floo-enss)—the place where two or more bodies of water flow together

density (DEN-sih-tee)—the amount of mass an object or substance has based on a unit of volume

Depression (di-PREH-shuhn)—the Great Depression was the deepest and longest-lasting economic downturn in the history of the Western industrialized world

engineer (en-juh-NEER)—a person who uses science and mathematics to design, build, or maintain machines, buildings, or public works

ferry (FER-ee)—a boat or ship that regularly carries people across a stretch of water

geologist (jee-AHL-uh-jist)—someone who studies minerals, rocks, and soil; geology is the study of how Earth was formed and how it changes

Gold Rush (GOLD RUSH)—the sudden arrival of crowds of people in search of gold

Ice Age (EYESS AJE)—a period of time when Earth was covered in ice; the last ice age ended about 11,500 years ago

primer (PRY-mur)—a base coat of paint that goes on before the main color

retrofit (reh-troh-FIT)—to provide something with new parts that were not available when it was originally built

rivet (RIV-it)—a strong metal bolt that is used to fasten something together

scaffolding (SKAF-ol-ding)—temporary framework or platforms used to support workers and materials

sheath (SHEETH)—a close-fitting cover for something, especially something that is elongated

strait (STRAYT)—a narrow channel of water that connects two larger bodies of water

union (YOON-yuhn)—a group of workers who try to gain more rights, such as fair pay and safer jobs, for workers

READ MORE

Hoena, Blake. *Building the Golden Gate Bridge.* North Mankato, Minn: Capstone Press, 2015.

Hurley, Michael. *The World's Most Amazing Bridges.* Landmark Top Tens. Chicago: Raintree, 2012.

Latham, Donna. *Bridges and Tunnels: Investigate Feats of Engineering.* White River Junction, Vt: Nomad Press, 2012.

Wearing, Judy, and Tom Riddolls. *Golden Gate Bridge.* New York: AV2, 2014.

INTERNET SITES

FactHound offers a safe, fun way to find Internet sites related to this book. All of the sites on FactHound have been researched by our staff.

Here's all you do:
Visit www.facthound.com
Type in this code: 9781491481967

CRITICAL THINKING USING THE COMMON CORE

1. Why was the south anchorage so much harder to build than the north anchorage? Cite evidence from the text to support your answer. (Key Ideas and Details)

2. Strauss' first bridge design incorporated cantilever elements. What is a cantilever bridge? (Craft and Structure)

3. The bridge tower's beehive cell structure allows it to sway in all four directions. Why is it important for the bridge to be able to do this? (Integration of Knowledge)

INDEX